Cats
Katzen

A dual language book
Ein zweisprachiges Buch

Selby Gunter

ISBN 9789083201177

First Edition, 2021

Written by Selby Gunter. Translated into German by Katharina Tränka. Cover and interior design by Natalia Junqueira and Selby Gunter. Photo credits Unsplash/The Lucky Neko, Jesús Boscán, Max Sandelin, Willian Justen de Vasconcellos, Chewy, Mel Elías, Süheyl Burak, Colours of Turkey, Roberto Jr Saldana, Sandra Kapella, Derek Sutton, zhang kaiyv, Timo Volz, Dietmar Ludmann, Milada Vigerova, Amber Kipp, Jane Duursma, Kanashi, Dorothea OLDANI, Paul Hanaoka, Christian Cacciamani, Alex Chambers, Tran Mau Tri Tam, Gerry Roarty, Darby P., Tucker Good, Milada Vigerova, The3dragons, Jason Leung, Aleksandra Sapozhnikova, ModCatShop, The Lucky Neko. Istock/cynoclub, Eriklam, jaqy, davit85, zsv3207, kimeveruss, AlenaPaulus.

Mona Cottage Publishing

Haarlem, Nederlands

www.monacottage.com

Contact publisher for wholesale orders.

Printed on demand. Country of print may vary.

Available Languages

English / Français

English / Deutch

English / Español

English / Nederlands

Share your language learning journey:

@monacottagepublishing

Mona Cottage Publishing

All cats start as kittens. They are born small but grow quickly.

Kittens are very curious and playful.

Kätzchen sind sehr neugierig und verspielt.

Some cats like to be held and pet.

Others do not like to be touched.

Andere mögen es nicht, wenn
man sie anfasst.

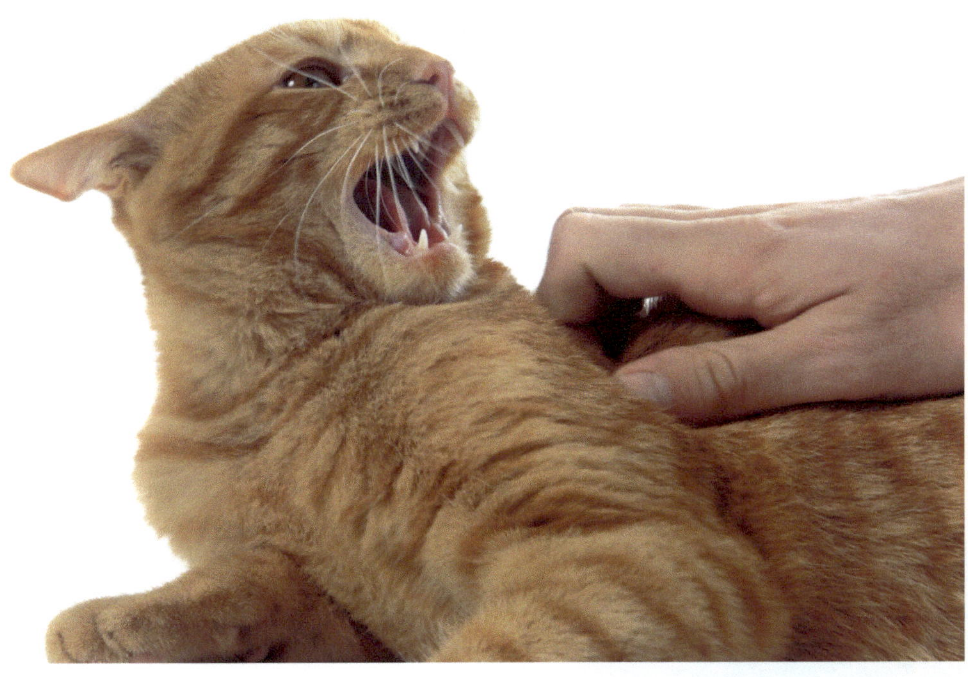

Cats are a popular pet.
Do you have a cat?

Katzen sind beliebte Haustiere.
Hast du eine Katze?

Cats live all over the world.

Katzen leben überall auf der Welt.

11

Cats come in many colors, sizes,
and fur types.

**Katzen gibt es in verschiedene
Farben, Größen und Fellarten.**

**Some cats are very fluffy.
They have long fur.**

**Manche Katzen sind sehr
flauschig. Sie haben langes Fell.**

13

Many cats have short fur.

Viele Katzen haben kurzes Fell.

But some have no fur at all!

Aber manche haben gar kein Fell!

Cats can have many different colors of fur.

Katzen können viele verschiedene
Fellfarben haben.

There are white, black, gray, and
orange cats.

Es gibt weiße, schwarze, graue und
orangene Katzen.

A cat can also be more than one color.

Eine Katze kann auch mehr als eine Farbe haben.

Cats can have stripes or spots.

Katzen können auch gestreift oder gefleckt sein.

And some have flat noses
or short legs.

Und manche haben ein flache Nase
und kurze Beine.

Cats are very good at jumping.
Many can jump over eight feet!

Katzen könne sehr gut springen.
Viele können über zwei Meter hoch springen!

25

They are also good hunters.
Cats hunt small animals and eat
mostly meat.

Sie sind auch gute Jäger. Katzen
können kleine Tiere jagen und sie
essen meistens Fleisch.

Cats like to play. They can be silly, funny, or sometimes naughty.

Katzen mögen es zu spielen. Sie können albern, lustig und manchmal auch frech sein.

Cats use their tongues to clean themselves. Do you clean yourself with your tongue?

Katzen benutzen ihre Zunge, um sich sauber zu machen. Machst du dich mit deiner Zunge sauber?

The foot of a cat is
called a paw. They
have four paws.

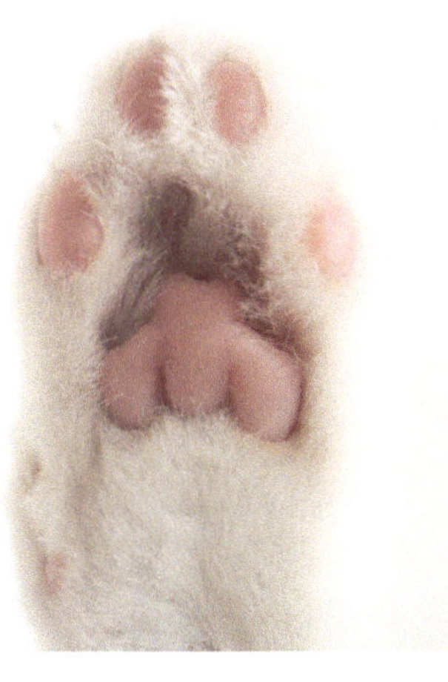

A cat's tail has many uses.

Der Schwanz von einer Katze hat viele Funktionen.

It can help the cat balance.

Er hilft der Katze das Gleichgewicht zu halten.

And it can also be used to communicate or talk to other cats.

Cats can also be lazy.
They like to sleep a lot.
Good night.

Katzen können auch faul sein.
Sie lieben es viel zu schlafen.
Gute Nacht.

Vocabulary- Wortschatz

Kitten - Kätzchen
Born - geboren
Curious - neugierig
Playful - verspielt
Popular - beliebte
To live - leben
World - Welt
Fluffy - flauschig
Fur - Fell
Short - gestreift
Stripes - strepen
Sports - gefleckt
Nose - Nase
To jump - springen
Hunters - Jäger
To play - spielen
Funny - komisch
Naughty - frech

Tongue - Zunge
Paw - Pfote
Tail - Schwanz
To communicate - kommunizieren
Lazy - faul
Good night - Gute Nacht

Check out more bilingual titles
and language combinations!

www.monacottage.com